The Ruins at Machu Picchu

by Sharon Gordon

Scott Foresman

Editorial Offices: Glenview, Illinois • New York, New York
Sales Offices: Reading, Massachusetts • Duluth, Georgia
Glenview, Illinois • Carrollton, Texas • Menlo Park, California

Picture a beautiful city set on a mountaintop, miles high in the air. Imagine this city filled with deep green landscape, magnificent waterfalls, and stone buildings that are as breathtaking as the classical structures of Europe. Now imagine this city is over four hundred years old and was home to the mighty Inca people. You have just discovered the ancient city of Machu Picchu in Peru, South America!

The Inca's amazing empire stretched from the Pacific Ocean on the west to the Amazon River Basin on the east. It included land in Colombia in the north, all the way to Chile in the south. Because it was so vast, the Incas called it the "Land of the Four Quarters."

For many hundreds of years, the Incas were just one of many native tribes living in this area. But by the 1200s they had moved into the Cuzco Valley. By the early 1500s, they controlled much of the land and had conquered the other native tribes. The Inca Empire lasted for a little over a hundred years. It ended in the 1500s when Spanish explorers began to arrive in South America. The Spanish forced the Incas off the ancient Inca land. Most of the Inca cities were destroyed, and along with them, much of their history and heritage.

That is why the discovery of the ancient ruins of Machu Picchu is so important. In 1911, Hiram Bingham, an archaeologist from the United States, came to Peru to learn about its past. He and others hoped to find and excavate ancient cities of the Incas. They had heard stories about incredible fortress cities hidden high up in the Andes Mountains.

Bingham and a Peruvian soldier began their exciting journey from the city of Cuzco. They started by exploring the area around the Urubamba River. As they traveled, they saw the ruins of many Inca villages. They also saw the ruins of temples and other stone buildings as they followed the river.

They passed an Inca quarry, where huge stones were cut and carved from the mountainside. These stones were used to make buildings throughout the empire. Bingham was amazed that the Incas were able to make such sturdy structures with no modern tools.

After a few days of travel, Bingham and his friend came upon a tiny village. They met a farmer who lived in a hut. He told them about some ruins he had seen and offered to show them the way.

It took the group a few days to get through the thick jungle and over the rugged mountain paths. They followed an old road to a high mountain ridge that was almost 8,000 feet above sea level. There sat the towering mountain peak of Machu Picchu, meaning "old peak."

Bingham had come upon a momentous discovery. It was the "Lost City of the Incas," unknown to the modern world. Bingham saw that there were amazing ruins at Machu Picchu. He sent workers in to start clearing a path to the city. Old bridges and crossings had to be repaired. Over four hundred years of weeds and vegetation had to be cut back!

During this time, Bingham went back to the United States to plan for a return trip to Machu Picchu. A year later, he and a team of archaeologists arrived at the site to study the ruins. They had to spend months digging out the brush and growth that covered the city and its buildings. They were especially careful to excavate tree roots that had grown in between the layers of stone of the structures.

Bingham knew right away that Machu Picchu was a fortress city. The Indians used it as a secret hideaway. Some think it might have been built to hide from the Spanish explorers. Or, it might have been constructed by the early Inca tribes to protect them from other enemies.

The reason Machu Picchu remained a secret for so long was that it was so hard to reach. Sitting on a mountaintop, it had steep slopes on all sides—too steep to climb. Only one side of the mountain could be used to make a path or road to the top. And the Incas made sure this single approach was carefully guarded! Here, the city was protected by colossal double walls—sixteen feet high and three feet thick. A dry moat was built in between the walls and around the city for extra protection. And, if that weren't enough, a giant gate made it enemy-proof!

A watchtower stood on the inside of the city gate. It was built on a giant stone slab. It had eight inner rooms with two windows that gave the Incas a good view of the valley below. From there, guards could see any enemy who approached the mountain city.

Because Machu Picchu was built into the side of a mountain, the city was made up of many different levels, or terraces. In between each of the terraces were stone stairways. Bingham and his team found over a hundred different stairways at Machu Picchu. Sometimes, several flights of stairs were carved out of one block of granite!

The leveled terraces got higher and higher until they reached the top of the city. The Incas grew crops and raised animals on the terraces. The terraces also helped save the city from erosion by wind and rain.

How did the Incas get all those large stones up the mountain? No one is certain. But it wasn't easy! Of course, some stones were found on the mountain. But others had to be brought up from distant quarries. Often, they had to be carried over the river and up steep paths.

Once the stones were brought to the proper place, they were cut and shaped by Inca stonecutters. These experts then used stone hammers and wet sand to polish the finished rock. The stones were moved into place by strong ropes and human strength. It's difficult to imagine the amount of time and effort it took to make a single dwelling.

Altogether, 143 stone buildings were found at Machu Picchu. About eighty of them were houses similar to those in other Inca cities. They were made of stone and had thatched roofs. Often, a group of homes surrounded an area where animals, such as llamas or goats, could graze. Other dwellings were located around areas where crops, such as corn or potatoes, could grow.

The remaining structures of Machu Picchu were palaces, temples, and places for special ceremonies. The Incas considered this mountain city to be sacred. At the very top of Machu Picchu was an area called the sacred plaza. It contained three separate temples: the great temple, the main temple, and a special house for the Inca priests.

The Incas believed in many gods, but the sun was the most important. They hoped this god would bring good weather and abundant crops. A special stone terrace with a tall clock-like top was found near the temple ruins. Many people believe it might have been a sundial. It probably helped the Incas keep track of the seasons, so that on June 21 they could celebrate the Festival of the Sun God.

Inside the main temple of Machu Picchu were three large windows in a unique shape. This shape, called a trapezoid, had four sides that became thinner at the top. Nearly all Inca buildings had this design, and it could be found in their doors and openings too.

Where did the Incas find fresh, flowing water to use up in their mountain homes? Hundreds of years before faucets and bottled water were invented, the Incas thought of a clever plan to bring water to their city.

They built a one-and-a-half-mile-long channel from the springs of a nearby peak into Machu Picchu. The channel crossed the moat that surrounded the city, ran under the city walls, and into what was called the "Stairway of Fountains." This was a series of stone basins which were connected by stairs. The spring water flowed from the top basin down through the different levels of the city. The Incas could bring their water jars to the basins to fill for drinking, cooking, cleaning, or bathing.

What is also amazing about Inca buildings is that the stones of their buildings were put in place without any mortar, or cement, to hold them together. Over all these years, the stone buildings have stood through all kinds of weather. In fact, the lack of mortar may have been a good thing. It may have protected their buildings from earthquakes, which occur quite often in the Andes Mountains. Because there was no cement holding them together, the stones were able to shift as the Earth shook.

Machu Picchu, like many other Inca cities, was carefully planned. There were special ways to care for all the citizens of the empire. There were structures for homes, for storing food, and even for storing fresh water. We must look with respect at the skilled workers who designed and built this mountain paradise one stone at a time.

Much of Machu Picchu has been restored and repaired. It is a wonderful place to see. Many of the old thatched-roof homes were rebuilt. Today these buildings give visitors a real sense of what it would have been like to live in this remote mountaintop city among the mighty Incas.